I'M GLAD THERE ARE...

Bees and Other Bugs

By **Tracey Turner** Illustrated by **Fiona Powers**

WINDMILL BOOKS

Published in 2025 by Windmill Books,
an Imprint of Rosen Publishing
2544 Clinton St.
Buffalo, NY 14224

First published in Great Britain in 2022 by The Watts Publishing Group

Credits
Design and project management: Raspberry Books
Art Direction and cover design: Sidonie Beresford-Browne
Design: Kathryn Davies
Illustration: Fiona Powers

Cataloging-in-Publication Data

Names: Turner, Tracey, author. | Powers, Fiona, illustrator.
Title: Bees and other bugs / by Tracey Turner, illustrated by Fiona Powers.
Description: Buffalo, New York : Windmill Books, 2025. | Series: I'm glad there are... | Includes glossary and index.
Identifiers: ISBN 9781538396285 (pbk.) | ISBN 9781538396292 (library bound) | ISBN 9781538396308 (ebook)
Subjects: LCSH: Bees--Juvenile literature. | Insects--Juvenile literature.
Classification: LCC QL565.2 T87 2025 | DDC 595.79'9--dc23

Printed in the United States of America
CPSIA Compliance Information: Batch #CSWM25: For Further Information contact Rosen Publishing at 1-800-237-9932

I'M GLAD THERE ARE...

Bees and Other Bugs

By **Tracey Turner** Illustrated by **Fiona Powers**

WINDMILL BOOKS

Contents

Chirp

I'M GLAD THERE ARE

Bees and Other Bugs

I LOVE BUGS! They can be beautiful, like butterflies or brightly colored beetles.

They can make a lovely sound, from the humming of a fuzzy bumblebee to the chirping of a cricket.

They can help our gardens grow. They are all amazing!

IN THIS BOOK you will meet different kinds of insects – including bees, beetles, and butterflies – and spiders. We're calling them all "bugs," like lots of people do, but a bug is really a special kind of insect.

Bugs are right on your doorstep, waiting for you to visit them. Just look and listen.

I'M GLAD THERE ARE

Bees

...because they're a sign that spring has come.

BEES start buzzing when the weather gets warmer and winter is over.

I like to watch bees as they fly from flower to flower, making their sleepy-sounding hum. There are lots of different kinds.

Bumblebees are the round, furry-looking ones.

Some kinds of bumblebee build their nests underground. Others nest in long grass, or in trees.

An energy drink for a tired bee

If you see a bee on the ground that isn't moving much, mix up two teaspoons of sugar with one teaspoon of water on a small plate, and put it right next to the bee. You might see the bee take a drink to give it the energy to fly away.

I'M GLAD THERE ARE

Honeybees

...because I love honey!

HONEYBEES buzz around collecting pollen and sucking up nectar from flowers. Back at their hive, they store the pollen for food, and use the nectar to make honey.

BEEKEEPERS keep bees in a hive, and take some of their honey for people to eat. They make sure the bees have enough for themselves.

By spreading pollen from one flower to another, bees help make seeds for new flowers. Lots of other bugs do this, too.

Help a honeybee

We can help honeybees by planting the flowers they like – lavender is a honeybee favorite. You don't have to have a garden, because bees are just as happy to visit a windowbox!

I'M GLAD THERE ARE Ants

...because they are clever animals.

There are THOUSANDS of different kinds of ants. They live together in big groups called colonies.

As ANTS wander about looking for food, they leave a chemical trail behind them that other ants can follow.

Ants can carry many times their own weight. If you were like an ant, you could carry a grown-up with no problem at all.

Ants are clever. Some farm little bugs called aphids, protect them from predators, and drink the honeydew the aphids make!

Lots of ants live in tropical forests, like these leaf-cutter ants from Central and South America. They snip bits off leaves with their sharp jaws, carry them back to the ant nest, then use them to grow a special fungus, which is the ants' food!

I'M GLAD THERE ARE

Butterflies

...because they are the most beautiful insects of all.

A BUTTERFLY'S brilliant colors can help it blend in with flowers, warn predators that it's not safe to eat, and attract other butterflies. The colors also make butterflies lovely to look at!

Butterfly young don't look at all like their parents.

Butterflies lay eggs (1), and caterpillars hatch from them (2). The caterpillar eats a lot, then turns into a pupa (3).

Then, inside the pupa, the butterfly grows and eventually comes out (4). When it's ready, it stretches out its wings and flies away (5). It's like magic!

Butterfly bushes

If you have a garden, you could ask to plant a buddleia plant (or "butterfly bush"), because butterflies love them. They have purple flowers and are easy to grow.

I'M GLAD THERE ARE

Crickets

...because they make a lovely summer sound.

Most CRICKETS come out and start to make their chirping song after the sun goes down.

Crickets make the sound by rubbing their wings together – the top of one wing scrapes across the bottom of the other wing. Only male crickets make the noise – they do it to attract female crickets.

Lots of crickets together make my favorite sound – a cricket choir! Maybe that's why people think these bugs bring good luck.

Make a bug hotel

To encourage crickets and all kinds of other bugs, make somewhere for them to shelter or lay their eggs. Use recycled plastic bottles with the front cut out and fill them with twigs, cardboard tubes, and dried-up flowers and leaves.

I'M GLAD THERE ARE Moths

...because they make the nighttime magical.

Most MOTHS come out at night, or at dawn and dusk. Some sniff out scented flowers and drink their nectar – they have a long, thin tube to reach inside flowers. Some moths don't eat at all, and others eat carpets and clothes!

This beautiful atlas moth is one of the biggest kinds of moths in the world. Its wingspan can be 12 inches (30 cm) – the size of a dinner plate! It lives in Southeast Asia. It's one of the moths that doesn't eat, but spends its short lifetime finding a mate and laying eggs.

There are other insects that don't eat when they're adults. Their energy comes from the food they ate as larvae.

I'M GLAD THERE ARE

Dragonflies

...because I love watching their acrobatic flight.

DRAGONFLIES are some of fastest flying insects, as they dart about hunting their prey. They can move backwards and sideways as well as forwards and up and down.

They have amazing bright colors. This one is a female emperor dragonfly.

Dragonflies often live near ponds because they lay their eggs in water. When they hatch, dragonfly larvae are fierce underwater predators before they become adult dragonflies.

Peer into a pond

Ponds attract lots of other insects, too – damselflies (like small dragonflies), water boatmen, and lots more. Go pond-watching with an adult and see how many bugs you can spot. You might see frogs and newts, too.

⚠ REMEMBER: always be careful near water!

I'M GLAD THERE ARE Beetles

...because they're incredible creatures.

There are hundreds of thousands of different types of BEETLES. If you made a list of all the different kinds of living things in the world, about one in every five would be some sort of beetle!

Ladybugs are beetles. They have two sets of wings – soft ones to fly, and hard ones like a shell that close over them. Most beetles have wings like this. I like the spots on a ladybug's hard outer wings.

Most beetles eat plants, but ladybugs eat smaller creatures. There are also creatures that eat them. If ladybugs think another animal is going to attack them, they can squirt poisonous chemicals from their legs!

Some beetles have gorgeous colors and patterns. Jewel beetles are shiny and come in bright colors, which confuses predators and makes the beetles harder for them to spot. This one is a multicolored beauty from Thailand.

I'M GLAD THERE ARE

Fireflies

...because they are like living fairy lights.

FIREFLIES twinkle on summer evenings using special light organs on their bodies. They flash on and off, just like lights on a Christmas tree.

Fireflies are a type of beetle. They light up the ends of their bodies to show one another where they are. There are about two thousand different kinds, and each kind has its own pattern of flashing lights!